D1490043

NL SNOWMAGEDDON 2020

NL SNOWMAGEDDON 2020

NICK CRANFORD

WITH A FOREWORD BY METEOROLOGIST EDDIE SHEERR

FLANKER PRESS LIMITED

ST. JOHN'S

Library and Archives Canada Cataloguing in Publication

Title: NL snowmageddon 2020 / Nick Cranford with a foreword by meteorologist Eddie Sheerr.
Other titles: Snowmageddon 2020 | Newfoundland and Labrador snowmageddon 2020
Names: Cranford, Nick, 1997- editor. | Sheerr, Eddie, writer of foreword.
Identifiers: Canadiana (print) 20200185098 | Canadiana (ebook) 20200185233 | ISBN 9781771177955
   (softcover) | ISBN 9781771177962 (PDF)
Subjects: LCSH: Blizzards—Newfoundland and Labrador—Pictorial works. | LCSH: Newfoundland and
   Labrador—History—21st century—Pictorial works.
Classification: LCC FC2178 .N5 2020 | DDC 971.8/050222—dc23

© 2020 by Nick Cranford

ALL RIGHTS RESERVED. No part of the work covered by the copyright hereon may be reproduced or used in any form or by any means—graphic, electronic or mechanical—without the written permission of the publisher. Any request for photocopying, recording, taping, or information storage and retrieval systems of any part of this book shall be directed to Access Copyright, The Canadian Copyright Licensing Agency, 1 Yonge Street, Suite 800, Toronto, ON M5E 1E5. This applies to classroom use as well.

PRINTED IN CANADA

Cover Design by Graham Blair   Interior Layout by Peter Hanes
Cover photos by Eric Aylward, Crystal Glynn, Vaida Nairn, Joles Alamares, Lori-Ann Smith, Katherine Wiseman Ryan,
Melanie Rebecca King, David Vere-Holloway, Government of Newfoundland and Labrador

FLANKER PRESS LTD.
PO BOX 2522, STATION C
ST. JOHN'S, NL
CANADA

TELEPHONE: (709) 739-4477   FAX: (709) 739-4420   TOLL-FREE: 1-866-739-4420

WWW.FLANKERPRESS.COM

9 8 7 6 5 4 3 2 1

We acknowledge the [financial] support of the Government of Canada. *Nous reconnaissons l'appui [financier] du gouvernement du Canada.* We acknowledge the support of the Canada Council for the Arts, which last year invested $153 million to bring the arts to Canadians throughout the country. *Nous remercions le Conseil des arts du Canada de son soutien. L'an dernier, le Conseil a investi 153 millions de dollars pour mettre de l'art dans la vie des Canadiennes et des Canadiens de tout le pays.* We acknowledge the financial support of the Government of Newfoundland and Labrador, Department of Tourism, Culture and Recreation for our publishing activities.

Dedicated to the memory
of Joshua Wall
(1994–2020)

Original artwork by Kyle Callahan Photography

"A lil something of the week we'll never forget, where we all came together and helped each other out."

CONTENTS

"The week of January 13, 2020, was primarily focused on the pending storm set to hit the province on Friday morning, the seventeenth: Will the seventy-five centimetres of snowfall be our reality? Say it ain't so. Will it miss us? Nobody knew for sure, but one of my favourite lines from the public is, 'Are the meteorologists just looking for clicks?' Or even better, 'Are the meteorologists in the pocket of Big Storm Chips?' Friday morning I was sitting in the studio hosting *Open Line* when Mayor Danny Breen joined us live to declare a state of emergency, and not a minute too soon. While totally breaking the rules, I hopped in the truck to get home to my family. Well, lo and behold, we got pummelled by seventy-five to ninety centimetres, accompanied by terrifyingly high winds to boot.

The following week was one of sore arms, broken backs, stir-crazy citizens, and joyous shovel brigades all over the region—heartwarming, to say the very least. As is our way, we are there for each other when times get tough (and of course with some complaining on *Open Line*). We won't soon forget Snowmageddon 2020."

— Paddy Daly, Host of VOCM *Open Line*

FOREWORD

BY METEOROLOGIST EDDIE SHEERR

The record-breaking blizzard, dubbed "Snowmageddon," that affected the Avalon Peninsula and northeastern Newfoundland on January 17 and 18, 2020, was one for the ages. This "weather bomb" is a storm that will be talked about for decades to come by the hundreds of thousands of people who lived through it. The rate at which the snow fell and intensity the wind blew was like nothing many had ever seen. And for Newfoundlanders to say that, it carries some weight. This storm was the single most intense weather event I've experienced. And as a meteorologist who grew up outside of Philadelphia, went to University in New Hampshire (Plymouth State University), lived in Georgia and Colorado, where I experienced severe weather and mountain blizzards, and finally resided in Newfoundland and Labrador the last six years, that, too, says something.

Any meteorologist gets excited when it comes to forecasting an extreme event. For many in the profession, it was an extreme weather event that hooked us on weather to begin with. For me, that obsession goes back as long as I can remember. Mostly it's been an obsession over snow. I love it. I can remember standing at the living room window at night as a little boy, with the lights off, peering outside looking for that first flake. My uncle Marc, upon seeing pictures and video of Snowmageddon, told me I was waiting by the window my whole life for a storm like this, and he couldn't have been more right.

This storm brought me back to my childhood. I think it brought a lot of people back to their childhoods. The city of St. John's was under a state of emergency for eight days. Kids were off from school for a week and got to be kids. Adults were off from work for a week and got to be kids! Seeing pictures of people enjoying the snow, sliding, making the coolest snow forts, and having neighbourhood campfires on the streets of St. John's showed me what Newfoundlanders do best—turn a hard time into a great time. Memories were made that will be talked about for a lifetime.

When forecasting this storm, the snowfall numbers showing in the data were jaw-dropping. In my experience, when data comes at you that's unbelievable, nine times out of ten, it is just that. Particularly when you're five to seven days out from a given event. However, when that data is shown by multiple computer models, for multiple days, you start to pay attention. Alarm bells start to go off. When the forecast is calling for 70 to 100 centimetres of snow and winds sustained over 100 kilometres an hour for hours on end, it's time to get serious. It's time to think about what the implications of such an event will be. Power outages, wind damage, and homes being quite literally snowed under are all things that came to mind in the days leading up to this. What didn't cross my mind was the logistical challenge of dealing with three feet or more of snow. How does one remove that amount? As it turns out, little by little. And with help. Help from neighbours and strangers, city and town workers, various municipalities, the provincial government, and even the military. This storm brought out the best in people. Brought out the true Newfoundland spirit that I've observed as a "come from away." Witnessing the aftermath of this storm made me proud to live on this rock in the North Atlantic. I love that I can call this place home.

Snowmageddon stats observed at St. John's International Airport

Consecutive hours of falling snow: 28
Consecutive hours of blizzard conditions: 18
Hours of wind sustained at 100 km/h or higher: 15

Peak wind speeds: 120–157 km/h
Most snow recorded in one hour: 10 cm (9:30–10:30 AM on January 17)
Snow recorded on January 17: 76.2 cm (new daily record!—previous 68.4 cm, April 5, 1999)
Total snow, January 17–18: 78 cm

Snowfall report from Environment Canada issued on January 19, 2020, at 3:00 PM NST

Mount Pearl: 93 cm
Paradise: 91 cm
St. John's East: 78 cm
Mount Carmel: 61 cm
Lethbridge: 48 cm
Gander International Airport: 35 cm
Gander West: 35 cm
St. Lawrence: 31 cm
Grand Falls–Windsor: 10 cm

Peak wind report from Environment Canada issued on January 19, 2020, at 3:00 PM NST

Green Island, Fortune Bay: 171 km/h
Bonavista: 164 km/h
Grates Cove: 156 km/h
Cape Pine: 146 km/h
Green Island, Trinity Bay: 145 km/h
Twillingate: 140 km/h
St. John's—Dohoney Place: 134 km/h
St. John's—East White Hills: 132 km/h
Saint Pierre: 130 km/h
St. John's Dockyard: 129 km/h
Pass Island: 126 km/h
Allan's Island: 116 km/h
Holyrood: 114 km/h
Bishop's Cove: 113 km/h
Ramea: 109 km/h
St. Lawrence: 106 km/h
Burgeo: 105 km/h
Deer Park: 101 km/h
Gander: 97 km/h

INTRODUCTION

Newfoundland and Labrador is an interesting place. We are a province blessed with many natural resources, a beauty unmatched by any other area on earth, and a people like no other. We've seen the sun shine on its brightest days and the rain fall on its darkest nights. But through it all, there was one common denominator: the will of the Newfoundlander. Newfoundlanders are not naive to the tests life throws our way. It is said adversity introduces a man to himself. We were introduced to that adversity once again on January 17, 2020.

That day, one of the worst blizzards in this province's history buried the eastern half of Newfoundland. Over 80 centimetres of snow fell in a single day. Hurricane-force winds picked up the snow and tossed it, reducing visibility to near zero. A state of emergency was declared in the capital city, St. John's, and lasted for eight days. The day after the storm, St. John's was entombed. It was like a scene out of the movie *The Day After Tomorrow*, in which New York City was buried in snow. This storm became forever known as "Snowmageddon."

Mother Nature gave us one of her heaviest punches yet, but what Mother Nature wasn't prepared for was its kryptonite: us. Out of the depths of that white stuff, we rose. Upon reflecting on this historic event, a question continued to linger in my mind and I'm certain for many as well: what is a Newfoundlander?

What defines us? Why were we able to handle this latest test with both grace and tenacity? I pondered day after day, trying to find the answer. The truth is, I couldn't find the answer. But I realized there is no single answer. There is no one-size-fits-all description of a Newfoundlander.

So, what is a Newfoundlander?

A Newfoundlander is someone who puts others' needs before their own. Living on an island, we've always had to rely on each other. Whether that was through shovelling your neighbour's driveway despite being exhausted after shovelling your own, donating food or clothing, driving a stranger to an urgent doctor's appointment or an essential worker to their shift in the middle of the state of emergency, or simply calling a family member or friend just to see if they're okay.

A Newfoundlander is someone who makes the best of a bad situation. Our late beloved friend Nevach Denine always said, "When life give you lemons, make lemonade." Well, life gave us snow, and we made it into a party. From the Georgetown block party to camping by a firepit made from snow, we sure had one heck of a time. To quote comedian Mark Critch, "Newfoundland is the only place where a disaster could strike and you'd wish you were there."

A Newfoundlander represents our government, whether that be at the federal, provincial, or municipal levels. Snowmageddon tested our limits. While we may have our differences politically, during the week-long state of emergency, we put them aside and worked toward one common goal: getting Newfoundland back on its feet. When all was said and done, we were able to rest easy, knowing that deep down in the middle of the chaos, we are all Newfoundlanders at heart who share a common goal: making Newfoundland the best place on earth.

And finally, a Newfoundlander represents our finest. They have forever embodied what it means to answer the call. We've seen that call answered by our nurses and doctors working days beyond the end of their scheduled shifts. We've seen that call answered by our equipment operators and power linemen working to exhaustion through the night to free our roads and get our heat and lights back on. We've seen that call answered by our firefighters, in particular, when they saved a family in the Battery who were buried by an avalanche. We've seen that call answered by our paramedics, who had to weather a maze of snow obstacles to get to the person they needed to save next. We've seen that call answered by our police officers, who made sure to respond to each call promptly. And we've seen that call answered by our men and women in uniform. In our time of need, the Canadian Army came to this province without hesitation and completed every task given to them without complaint. From the bottom of our hearts, we say thank you.

Those are just some of the things that make a Newfoundlander. The bottom line is that a Newfoundlander is who we are. It's all of the traits that make us unique. Newfoundland and Labrador is not the difference between an island and the Mainland or the battle for our bountiful resources. Newfoundland and Labrador is a vision for what the rest of the world can be. Graydon Pelley, Leader of the NL Alliance Party, quite aptly said that, during Snowmageddon, we saw the greatest in humanity.

What you will see in the pictures throughout this book is the story of our incredible tale. Each page represents a story in itself while also illustrating the definition of the Newfoundlander. While Snowmageddon brought some heartache and unimaginable stress, it also brought many blessings. We made new friendships, we helped one another, we managed to keep one of our new year's resolutions thanks to all of that shovelling, we had a laugh, and we've made memories that will last a lifetime. And to top it all off, Snowmageddon blessed us with a newborn child: Levi "Baby" Snow. Can anything be more fitting?

We passed Mother Nature's latest test with highest honours. There will be many others, but there is no doubt Newfoundlanders will pass the next one as well.

To our neighbourhoods. To our communities. To our great province. And, most importantly, to Newfoundlanders one and all.

Enjoy the book!

Nick Cranford

PREVIOUS PAGE: Original artwork by Joy Hecht

"What do you do when there's a massive blizzard and the city is in a state of emergency for eight days, with everything closed and no place to go?

Art, of course!

This is the view out my window on Lime Street. The storm brought out the best in my neighbours. We all grabbed our shovels, not only to clear our own doorways and cars but to dig each other out. I finally met the man in the red house down the street, and a young fellow in a white house up the hill. I got to know the Nigerian nurse in the green house, whose red car was completely hidden under an eight-foot drift before we all chipped in and spent hours clearing the snow around it. I may have even gotten on the good side of the woman across the street and her husband, whom I thought had never liked me!"

Cochrane Street, St. John's,
during the storm, January 18 (Jane Burry)

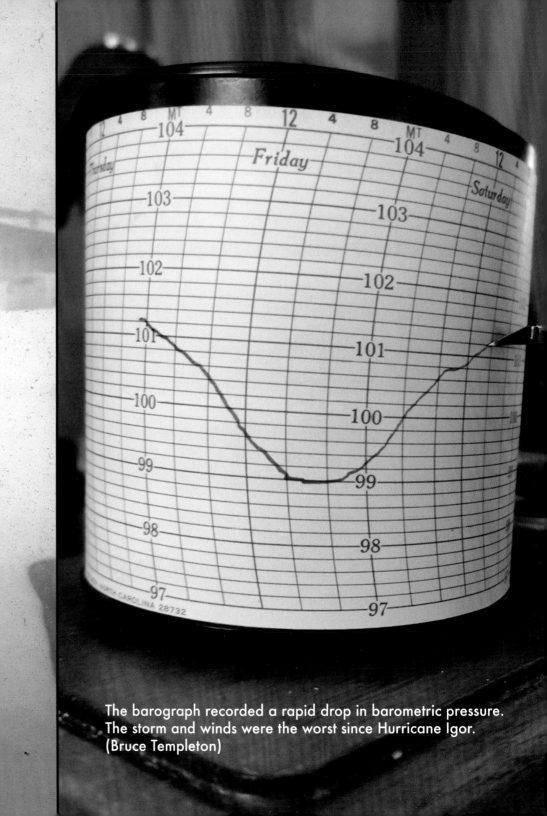

Vancouver Street, St. John's, early afternoon during the storm (Robin Wiseman)

The barograph recorded a rapid drop in barometric pressure. The storm and winds were the worst since Hurricane Igor. (Bruce Templeton)

Church Road, Conception Bay South,
9:00 PM, January 17 (Theresa Gormley)

Bus stop, St. John's (Erik McLean)

"All we can do now is hibernate." Photo taken in Paradise. (Kim Porter)

An angry ocean after the storm, Pouch Cove
(Alicia Sainsbury)

Buried in snowdrifts, St. John's
(Heather Corkum)

Fox Avenue, St. John's
(Heather Green Samson)

The intersection of Patrick Street and Hamilton Avenue, St. John's (Michelle Power)

St. John's harbourfront with Cabot Tower visible in the background (Karen Smith Photography)

A snowy doorway in St. John's (Erik McLean)

Aerial view, St. John's (Eric Aylward)

Photo taken in St. John's (Donna Coish)

"At home in Kilbride during a twenty-hour power outage, January 17" (Janice Williams)

Church Road, Conception Bay South, during the storm (Theresa Gormley)

View from Battery Road, St. John's
(Annette Dale Michelin)

Photo taken in Paradise (Lori-Ann Smith)

Mount Pearl the night of the storm (Lawrence Mak)

St. John's (Eric Aylward)

Prince Philip Drive, St. John's (Robert Dale)

A snowed-in snow door on Vancouver Street, St. John's (Robin Wiseman)

Photo taken in St. John's (Donna Coish)

A buried house on Green Acre Drive, St. John's
(Thelma Reid)

Photo taken in St. John's
(Cass Williams)

Photo taken in Shea Heights, St. John's
(Sean Vinnicombe)

"Missing: One basement door," Cowan Heights, St. John's (Fallon Faulkner)

Master Corporal Batten of 37 Signal Regiment found his army truck like this at Garrison, St. John's. (Corporal Kellie Cluney)

Photo taken in Paradise (James Hennessey)

Edgecombe Drive, St. John's (Courtney Snow)

Wind damage in Pouch Cove after the storm (Alicia Sainsbury)

Edgecombe Drive, St. John's (Courtney Snow)

Helping to excavate a neighbour's car on Maxse Street, St. John's, January 18 (Maria Lear)

Water Street, St. John's (Cahill Carew)

Trapper John's, George Street, St. John's (Karen Smith Photography)

Downtown St. John's (Vaida Nairn)

Leslie Street, St. John's (Kathleen Hickey)

Water Street, St. John's (Karen Smith Photography)

Photo taken in St. John's
(Vaida Nairn)

Downtown St. John's (Alick Tsui)

Monroe Street, St. John's (Danielle Goldsworthy)

Monroe Street, St. John's (Danielle Goldsworthy)

"Our old Victorian house on Patrick Street, St. John's" (Michelle Power)

Health Sciences Centre, emergency entrance, during the storm, St. John's (Sandra Sweetland)

Doyle Street, Brookfield Estates, St. John's (Perry Gould)

Dowdens Road, Seal Cove, Conception Bay South,
a week after the snowstorm (Angela Delaney)

Easy Listening
"and the music of your life"
Broadcasting Since 1924

Michelle Power on top of the snowbank touching the street's walk lights, Patrick Street, St. John's (Michael Ryan)

St. John's (Erik McLean)

The walking trail (train tracks) from Pond Road headed east, Kelligrews, Conception Bay South (Kerilyn Percy-Baldwin)

Tracy Fowler at her parents' house contemplating with her father, Albert, where to start, Newfoundland Drive, St. John's (Tracy Fowler)

"Walking our two potbelly pigs, Charlie and Teaspoon, to the barn for the day, Brookfield Road, 9:00 AM, January 17" (Dena Eales)

The day after the storm, Faulkner Street, St. John's (Joles Alamares)

Bluebell Bend, St. Philip's
(Jim Burton)

St. John's
(Mike Hennessey)

View from the cloverleaf, St. John's (Shawn Roche)

"Quite a snowdrift," St. John's (Jacinda Bennett)

St. John's (Mike Hennessey)

St. John's (Erik McLean)

Photo taken in Paradise (Lori-Ann Smith)

Mount Pearl (Lawrence Mak)

Cars stranded in snow, Rotary Drive, St. John's (Jenna Smith)

Highland Drive, St. John's (Melanie Rebecca King)

A young boy enjoys the day after the snow has settled, Mobile (Charlene Power)

An evening stroll after the storm was picture perfect as the sun set over Mobile Bay. Storm surges followed by a deep cold left the rocks ice-covered. (Charlene Power)

High sea swells crash against the shores of Mobile (Charlene Power)

Photo taken at the corner of Lodge Road and Concord Drive, Foxtrap (Shalane Lewis)

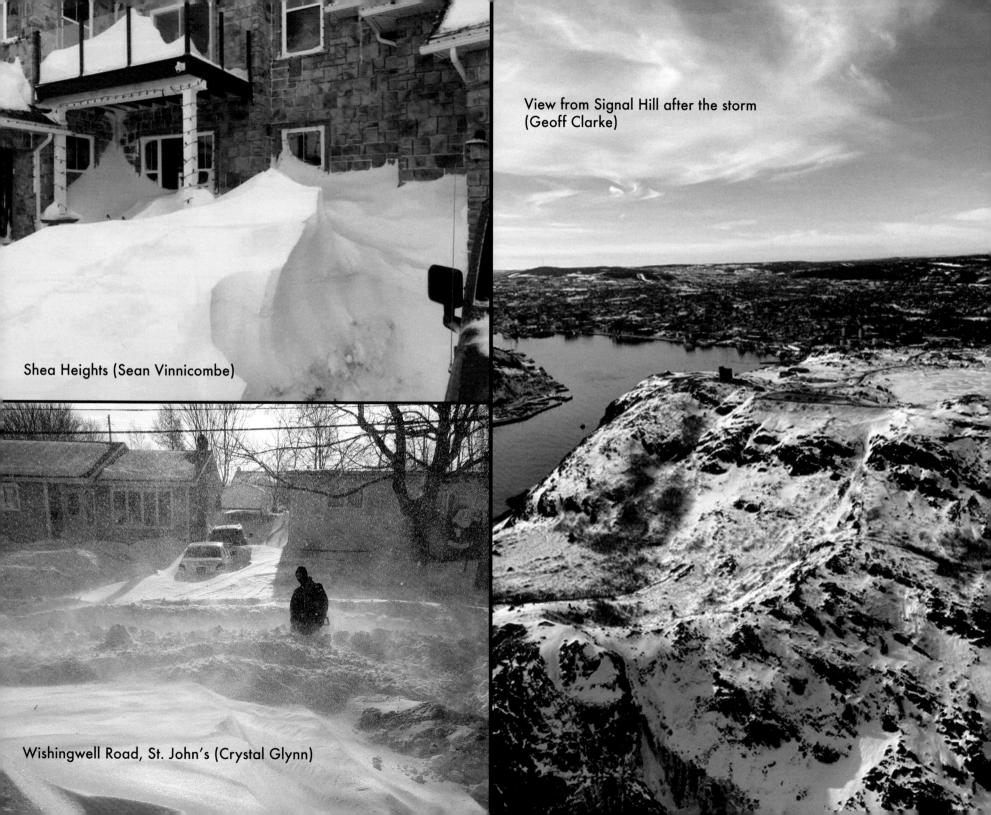

Shea Heights (Sean Vinnicombe)

Wishingwell Road, St. John's (Crystal Glynn)

View from Signal Hill after the storm (Geoff Clarke)

St. John's
(Crystal Glynn)

Highland Drive, St. John's (Melanie Rebecca King)

Highland Drive, St. John's (Melanie Rebecca King)

Beaumont Street, St. John's (Jonathan Wells Photography)

Campbell Avenue, St. John's (Jonathan Wells Photography)

Beaumont Street, St. John's (Jonathan Wells Photography)

Beaumont Street, St. John's (Jonathan Wells Photography)

St. John's after the storm
(Nicholas Brake)

St. John's
(Alick Tsui)

Wishingwell Road, St. John's
(Crystal Glynn)

Joanne Pretty taking a rest after day two of shovelling, Mount Pearl (Joanne Pretty)

Paradise (Lori-Ann Smith)

Paradise (Lori-Ann Smith)

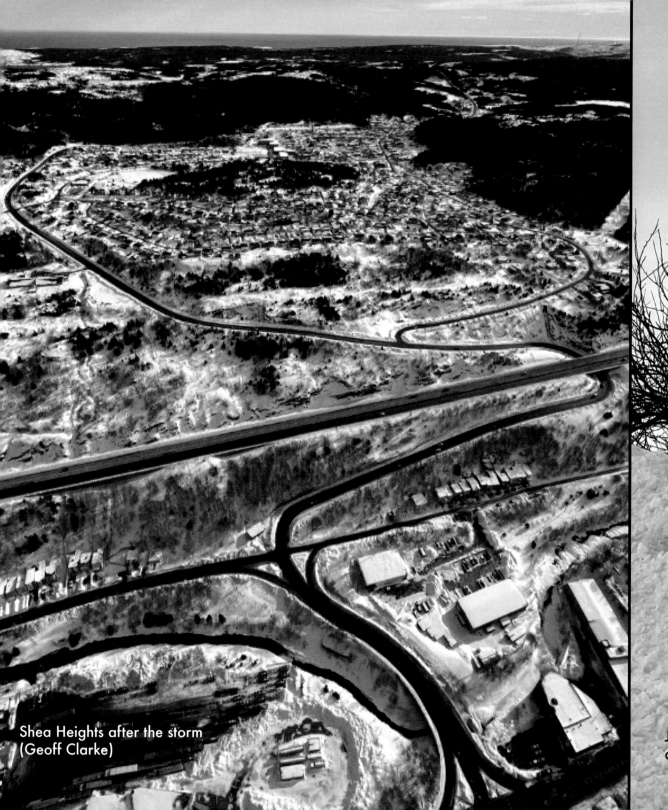

Shea Heights after the storm
(Geoff Clarke)

Julie Sinnott, "Queen of Gardiner," Gardiner Place, St. John's (Yuri Muzychka)

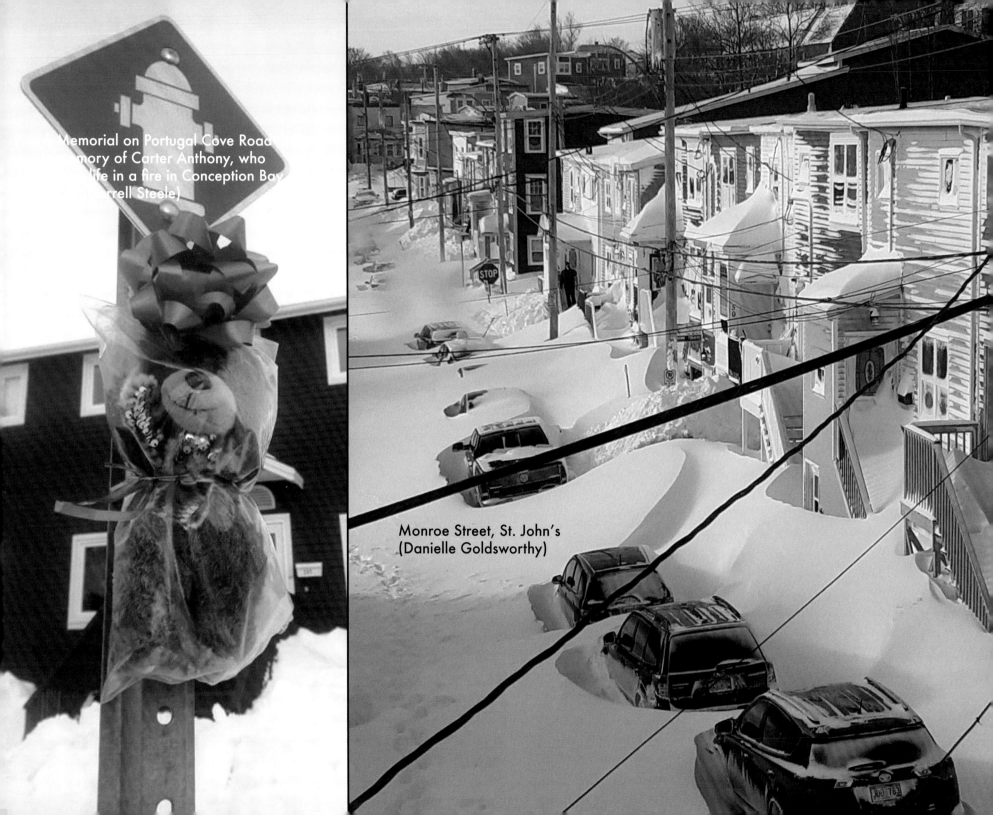

Memorial on Portugal Cove Road,
memory of Carter Anthony, who
life in a fire in Conception Bay
rrell Steele)

Monroe Street, St. John's
(Danielle Goldsworthy)

Montague Street, St. John's (Brenda Power)

Neighbours on Fair Haven Place helping one another (Trina Russell)

Clearing snow in St. John's (Tyler Pardy)

Bellevue Crescent, Cowan Heights,
St. John's (Kayla Howard)

Leslie Street, St. John's (Kathleen Hickey)

A backhoe digs out a snowy driveway in
St. Philip's (Janet Martin)

Canadian Army personnel digging out seniors on Hoyles Avenue, St. John's (Ramona Sturge)

"Remember to roll up your windows before a storm!" Smallwood Drive, Mount Pearl. (John Riche)

"He is 6'3 and there are two cars under there somewhere," Goulds (Joanne McDonald)

Hours upon hours of plowing in Southlands (Maddie Janes)

Photo taken in Southlands (Sean Vinnicombe)

Bellevue Crescent, Cowan Heights, St. John's (Kayla Howard)

View from the cloverleaf, St. John's (Shawn Roche)

Mount Pearl (Lawrence Mak)

Snow wall in Galway, January 23 (Annmarie Ottenheimer)

"Many hands make light work," Salmonier Place, St. John's (Melanie Byrne)

Snow piled five feet high on a 100-foot-long driveway makes a long day for Warren, Wayne, and Joel Eason, Raven Place, Conception Bay South (Valeria Eason)

Four days later, still trying to get to the road, corner of Cormack and Perlin, St. John's (Diane Power)

St. John's (Alick Tsui)

Perry Kendall digs his way to the shed to get to his snow-blower, Christine Crescent, Paradise (Cecilia Abuque)

Old Pennywell Road, St. John's. A loader clears access to refuel a generator on a tower site for essential service communications, January 18. (Nicole Martin)

Thankful to be freed by a Good Samaritan, St. John's (Heather Corkum)

St. John's (Alick Tsui)

St. John's (Vaida Nairn)

Digging out an older lady who was trapped in her basement apartment for two days, St. John's (Jacinda Bennett)

Stephen Martin takes a shovel to make sure his potbelly pigs can make it to barn. The loader can only get so much. Brookfield Road, St. John's, January 18 (Dena Eales)

Kilbride (Mike Hearn and Melanie O'Brien)

Health Sciences Centre, St. John's (Sandra Sweetland)

Health Sciences Centre, St. John's, two days after the snowstorm (Sandra Sweetland)

Snow removal in St. John's (Michelle Power)

St. John's (Alick Tsui)

Mount Pearl (Kim Losinski)

Flirt the dog heads to the supermarket with her grocery bag after the state of emergency was lifted. (Elaine Simmons)

St. John's (Karen Smith Photography)

Fox Avenue, St. John's (Heather Green Samson)

Wishingwell Road, St. John's (Crystal Glynn)

Ropewalk Lane and Mundy Pond Road, St. John's (Jonathan Wells Photography)

Melanie Rebecca King clears a neighbour's driveway on Highland Drive, St. John's (David Vere-Holloway)

Fox Avenue, St. John's (Heather Green Samson)

Highland Drive, St. John's (Melanie Rebecca King)

Corner of Dunlea Street and Birchwynd Street,
Wedgewood Park, St. John's (Melanie Rebecca King)

St. John's (Crystal Glynn)

Cleanup on Beaumont Street, St. John's (Jonathan Wells Photography)

Corner of Campbell Avenue and Ropewalk Lane, St. John's (Jonathan Wells Photography)

Kenmount Terrace, St. John's, during the state of emergency (Brad Wade, Asterix Droneworks)

Cashin Avenue, St. John's
(Jonathan Wells Photography)

Wishingwell Road, St. John's
(Crystal Glynn)

"Found the basement door!"
Cowan Heights, St. John's (Fallon Faulkner)

Mount Pearl, January 17 (Peter Hanes)

Snowdrift on Church Road, Conception Bay South, 10:00 AM, January 18 (Theresa Gormley)

Mount Pearl, January 18, the morning after (Peter Hanes)

Major's Path, St. John's (Bobby Smith)

Paradise (James Hennessey)

Looking down Brentwood Drive, Thorburn Woods Subdivision, St. Philip's (Janet Martin)

Montague Street, St. John's (Brenda Power)

William Tan after neighbours and family helped dig him and his wife out, St. John's (Katyana Tan)

Leslie Street, St. John's (Wendy Koh)

Old Petty Harbour Road, St. John's (Dandan Flores)

St. John's (Karen Smith Photography)

St. John's (Karen Smith Photography)

Forest Road, St. John's
(Sharron Forristall)

Monroe Street, St. John's
(Danielle Goldsworthy)

St. John's (Jacinda Bennett)

St. John's (Melissa Nolan)

2 — Beyond the Overpass

PREVIOUS PAGE: Original painting by Sarah Brazil

"A Chance of Snow"

Painted in fond remembrance of Snowmageddon 2020

A front step topples during the storm, Carbonear (Kaitlyn Somerton)

Placentia (Marjorie Lockyer Hancock)

West Loop Road, Gaskiers (Colleen Critch)

A snow-covered driveway in Harbour Grace (Brianne Jordan)

Carbonear (Melissa O'Keefe)

New Harbour, Trinity Bay
(Glendalynn Cranford)

Sealers Memorial in Elliston after the storm.
Photo by Neil Tucker. (Bruce Templeton)

Brianne and Christopher Jordan finally married in Harbour Grace on January 18, during the state of emergency (Brianne Jordan)

Brianne, Christopher, and Father Emmanuel, who went above and beyond to get them married in Harbour Grace(Brianne Jordan)

"Right back to shovelling for our honeymoon" (Brianne Jordan)

Bridal party in Harbour Grace: Teri-Lynn, Amanda, Brianne, Christopher, Mitchell, Edmund (Brianne Jordan)

Greenhouse covered with eight feet of snow, Riverhead, St. Mary's Bay (Mary Comerford)

Tors Cove (Michelle Power)

Holyrood (Brendan Power)

New Harbour, Trinity Bay (Glendalynn Cranford)

During the night of the storm, residents of Colliers heard an eerie banging noise. All through the night it was like a terrible drum. When the residents woke the next day, they found that an abandoned vessel had broken from its mooring lines and drifted around the harbour, finding a new resting place—against a massive rock just off shore. (Brad Wade, Asterix Droneworks)

Tilton (Colleen Richards Gosse)

Tors Cove (Michelle Power)

Victoria (Elsie Parsons-Collins)

Bay Roberts (Deanna Baker)

Bay Roberts (Michele Nicholson)

3 —
HAVE FUN
WILL SHOVEL

PREVIOUS PAGE: Original artwork by Seth Morgan

Seven-year-old Seth Morgan's painting went viral on Facebook following Snowmageddon, and now his artwork is being printed on T-shirts, with all proceeds going to the Gathering Place, a non-profit in St. John's. Julia Halfyard, Seth's mother, said the painting was first posted on a popular Facebook group, "NL Snowmageddon 2020 Warriors," created by Nick Cranford, which came together during the January blizzard and exploded with membership from all over the world as curious onlookers kept up to date with happenings in Newfoundland after one of the worst storms in the island's recent history.

Caleb and Kyla from Torbay (Ashley Wells-Newhook)

Beckett and Brooks Morgan in Paradise
(Samantha Morgan)

Caleb and Kyla from Torbay (Ashley Wells-Newhook)

Elsa in Kenmount Terrace, St. John's (Eliza King)

Melanie Rebecca King smiles after a shopper kindly gave her two of her own potatoes when the local grocery store ran out of supplies, St. John's (Melanie Rebecca King)

Westminster Drive, Mount Pearl (Shane Follett)

Original artwork by Emily Hunt

"Breakthrough! Great job, Sarah and Alexa Fowler!"
Penney Crescent, St. John's. (Tracy Fowler)

Tonie Keats hangs from a basketball net that is ten feet off the ground (Karen Hurley)

The Canadian Army saves the day in Cowan Heights, St. John's (Carolann Harris)

Matthew, seven, asked his mom if he could help the soldiers shovel snow. As he had cerebral palsy, getting outside was impossible. The military saw the social media post from Matthew's mother, Lisa, and paid them a visit in St. John's. (Lisa Sharpe)

Matthew with Canadian Army personnel (Lisa Sharpe)

Corporal Kellie Cluney, 37 Signal Regiment, shares chocolates with children on Bell Island (Corporal Kellie Cluney)

"Chewy the dog was excited to see the 4th Artillery Regiment after being trapped for four days in our home." (Kim Tremblett)

Thank you Troops for All your Service!

(Crystal Glynn)

Thank you so much for coming to Newfoundland and helping people dig out from Snowmageddon 2020

Love: Ashley

Thank You for all your service and for coming to help!

#Snowmageddon2020

(Crystal Glynn)

(Crystal Glynn)

(Crystal Glynn)

People line up outside local grocery stores to restock when the state of emergency is temporarily lifted (Crystal Glynn)

(Crystal Glynn)

PRODUCT OF NEWFOUNDLAND

7⁴⁹

Hungry people wait in line at Memorial Dominion, Quidi Vidi Lake, St. John's (Dana Healey)

Memorial Dominion, Quidi Vidi Lake, St. John's (Dana Healey)

Sobeys, Merrymeeting Road, St. John's, January 21 (Maria Lear)

"Light at the end of the tunnel," Cowan Heights, St. John's (Fallon Faulkner)

Seven-year-old Ryan Marsh on his front lawn on Palm Drive, Southlands, St. John's (Kim Marsh)

Salmonier Place, St. John's (Melanie Byrne)

Christine Lilly's thirteen-year-old son learns how to bake bread during the storm, St. John's (Christine Lilly)

Susan Moore Piercey sits for a spell in snow that needs to be cleared, Highland Drive, St. John's (Melanie Rebecca King)

Dialysis nurses are still smiling as they leave a weekend-long shift at the Health Sciences Centre, St. John's: Lori Roche, Courtney Norris, Janice Holwell, Linda Elms (Lori Roche)

Nanci Corcoran's daughter Nora after the storm, Seal Cove, Conception Bay South (Nanci Corcoran)

Workers stand on three feet of snow outside Memorial Dominion, Quidi Vidi Lake, St. John's, January 19 (Shawn Roche)

100 centimetres of snow in Portugal Cove (Kim Shannahan)

"Maple syrup is the key to survival," Freshwater Road, St. John's (Omar Farooq Rahman)

Georgina Street, Kenmount Terrace, St. John's (Desiree Walters)

Neighbours of Darcy Street enjoying a fire and treats during the state of emergency (Tammy Bishop)

The calm after the storm, Cowan Heights, St. John's (Fallon Faulkner)

(Carissa Lockyer)

After the storm, "Newfoundland Strong" (Carla Pilgrim Mulrooney)

St. John's (Andrea Sullivan)

All warm and cozy, Cowan Heights, St. John's (Fallon Faulkner)

Ridgewood Drive, Paradise (Eileen Woodford)

Spruce, a rescue from Labrador, in Pouch Cove (Rhoda English)

St. John's (Andrea Sullivan)

(Deon Dyke)

Sarah Fowler at home on Penney Crescent (Tracy Fowler)

Maddie Wareham and her father, Matthew Wareham, Fox Farm, Carbonear (Holly Wareham)

Hard at work, Cowan Heights, St. John's (Fallon Faulkner)

Jess Fahey: "When in doubt, build a snow fort" (Nick Hunt)

Acharya Drive, Paradise (Ashley Major)

"Helping out the elderly brings family together." Clovelly, St. John's. (Caroline Grant)

I Survived SNOWMAGEDDON 2020

(Terry Scott, memoriestolast.com)

Georgina Street, Kenmount Terrace, St. John's (Desiree Walters)

(Erik McLean)

St. John's, January 20 (Vaida Nairn)

St. John's (Karen Smith Photography)

Five-month-old Max John is not impressed with the snow. (Jennifer Sparkes)

"It is fit for a polar bear outside!" (Kathryn Oliver)

Two-and-a-half-year-old Alexa and her grandma make homemade bread in anticipation of a power outage, Newfoundland Drive, St. John's (Tracy Fowler)

Victoria, Newfoundland (Pauline Snook)

Sadie is having a ball making a sliding spot in her driveway in Conception Bay South, January 18 (Theresa Gormley)

(Trudy Puddicombe)

(Terry Scott, memoriestolast.com)

Scooby the dog now has a state-of-the-art
doggy snow outhouse (Kim Porter)

Cochrane Street, St. John's (Jane Burr

Skiing on Cochrane Street, St. John's, January 18 (Jane Burry)

Cashin Avenue (Jonathan Wells Photography)

St. John's
(Alick Tsui)

St. John's
(Alick Tsui)

St. John's (Karen Smith Photography)

(Elsie Parsons-Collins)

Salmonier Place, St. John's (Melanie Byrne)

"Having a scoff" in Paradise (Kyle Jones)

David Cooney enjoying a cold one, Rabbittown, St. John's (Ashley Cooney)

St. John's (Nicholas Perry)

St. John's (Karen Smith Photography)

St. John's, January 20 (Vaida Nairn)

Lineup outside Caines, Duckworth Street, St. John's (Vaida Nairn)

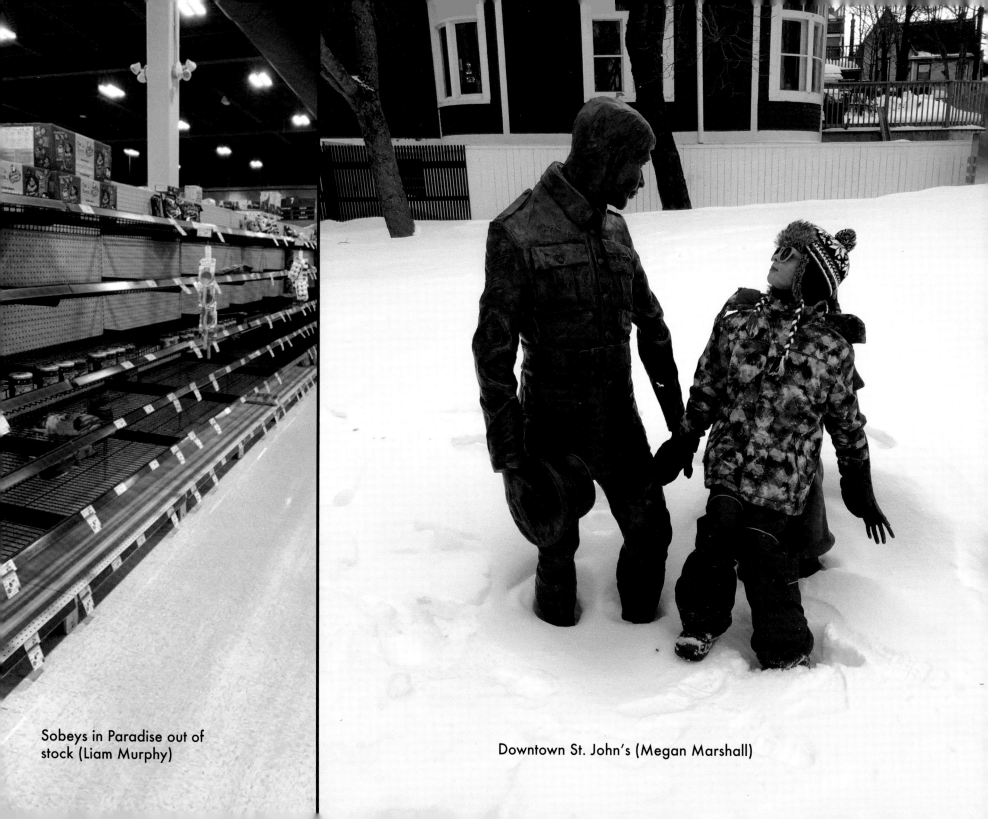

Sobeys in Paradise out of stock (Liam Murphy)

Downtown St. John's (Megan Marshall)

Downtown St. John's (Megan Marshall)

John Pippy of Pouch Cove (Rhoda English)

Sheena King takes her puppy, Rufus, outside to do his business after twenty-four hours of holding it in, Chapman Crescent, St. John's, January 18 (Sheena King)

Snowmobilers on Atlantica Drive, Paradise, January 18 (Shawn Roche)

Firemen on Cochrane Street, St. John's, January 18 (Jane Burry)

St. John's (Megan Marshall)

St. John's (Mike Hennessey)

St. John's (Andrea Sullivan)

WARM WINTER WISH

Photo taken in Carbonear (Ivy Lehr)

(Amy Fifield)

Sixteen-year-old Nicholas Hallett shovels all week for his grandmother on Fourth Street, Mount Pearl (Melanie Hallett)

(Samantha Banton)

"Finally reached the road! Now we're throwing snow into the snowblower." Cormack Street, St. John's. (Diane Power)

Canadian Army personnel shovel Lime Street, St. John's (Susan Stuckless)

Mount Pearl (Kim Losinski)

Garry Cranford shovels snow in his driveway on Canada Drive, Cowan Heights, St. John's (Nate & Nicole Photography)

Skiing in St. John's (Nate & Nicole Photography)

Downtown St. John's (Nate & Nicole Photography)

Levi Jacob Snow, born during the snowstorm on January 17 (Kyle Snow)

(Nate & Nicole Photography)

(Nate & Nicole Photography)

ACKNOWLEDGEMENTS

The author would like to thank the volunteer administrators and moderators whose help was instrumental in making the Facebook group "NL Snowmageddon 2020 Warriors" a success. A special thank you to Geoff Clarke, Jerry Cranford, Nick Hillier, Jennifer Hiscock, Bev A. Morgan, Carolyn R. Parsons, and Char Squires.

In addition, the author and the publisher would like to give heartfelt thanks to the following people who contributed photos and so much more to this book and without whom it would not have been possible to publish. While space limited us from using all the images that were submitted, we greatly appreciate each and every person who reached out to Flanker Press for this project. Thank you all:

Cecilia Abuque, Lamia Urshan Ahmed, Joles Alamares, Mostafa Alkhunaizi, Michael Allen, Holly Ann, David Ash, Nikki Ashley, Ada Augot, Eric Aylward, Deanna Baker, Dominique Baker, Kathy Baker, Heather Balson-Tobin, Samantha Banton, Eliza Barrett, Carol Belliveau, Jacinda Bennett, Viola Benson, Lucille Beresford Pumphrey, Lorelei Best, Marion Biles, Megan Bishop, Tammy Bishop, Della Bolt, Carol Bradbury, Julia Brake, Nicholas Brake, Judy Marie Brazil, Sarah Brazil, Danny Breen, Margaret Breen Earle, Linda Browne, Kim Bungay Marsh, Ashley Lola Burgess, James Burke, Jane Burry, Melanie Burry, Jess Burton, Jillian Burton, Colleen Bussey, Michelle Butler-Greeley, Matt Butt, Melanie Byrne, Phil Byrne, Teresa Caines Cox, Kyle Callahan, Maxwell Canning, Tammy Canning, Cahill Carew, Alice Marie Carroll, Jarratt Carter, Lorie Carter, HJ Cayuse, Marlaina Chafe, Trudy Chafe, Sean Churchill, Elizabeth Clairmont, Marjorie Clarke, Suzanne Clarke, Roman Clowe, Kellie Cluney, Donna Coish, Cathy Collins, Sonya L. Collins, Deanne Collins Chipman, Mary Comerford, Ashley Cooney, David Cooney, Melissa Cooper, Nanci Corcoran, Lorraine Courvoisier, Glendalynn Cranford, Kelly Cribb, Colleen Critch, Steve Crocker, Jillian Croke Ackerman, Doreen Cromwell, Bonnie Curnew Hyde, Robert Dale, Paddy Daly, Brent Dawe, Annette June Dearing, Dana Decker, Madonna Delaney, Scosha Diamond, Ben Dingle, Kat Drover, Maria Drover, Karen Duff Walters, Kim Dunne, Joanne Dunne Glassman, Deon Dyke, Dena Eales, Marylee Earle-Janes, Joel Eason, Monica Eason, Valeria Eason, Warren Eason, Wayne Eason, Stephanie Edwards, Jennifer Elizabeth, Rhoda English, Tonia Evans, Bernice Evans-Hillier, Marina Eveleigh, Robyn Eveleigh King, Jesse Fagan, Jessica Fagan, Jess Fahey, Fallon Faulkner, Shazza Fazza, Amy Fifield, Martine Fillion, Cliff Finney, Charmaine Fitzgerald, Aaron Flood, Dandan Flores, Nora Ford, Tracy Fowler, Scott Fowlow, Wayne Fraser, Nikki Furlong Martin, Samantha Gallie, Stacey Garland, Natosha Gillam, Jo Gunny Gilliland, Stephen Glassman, Crystal Glynn, Danielle Goldsworthy, Heather Gordon, Caroline Grant, Terri Green, Wayne Greene, Heather Green Samson, Jillian Kathleen Greenslade, Kim Griffin, Courtney Griffiths, Kevin Haley, Maria Halfyard, Sherry Halleran, Melanie Hallett, Samantha Hallett, Kassidy Hammond, Janessa Hand, Julie Hanlon, Lisa Ann Marie Hanlon, Peggy Hann, Robyn Hannam, Ashley Harding, Carolann Harris, Fred Harris, Noel Harris, Edgar Hartling, Dana Healey, Mike Hearn, Joy Hecht, Mike Hennessey, Paula Hennessey, Kathleen Hickey, Bernice Hillier, Lisa Hinchey, Amanda Hogan, Paula Holloway Ash, Jo-Anne Nichole Holwell, Kayla Howard, Rachel Hoyles, Jessica Hua Ayles, Adam Hulan, Dean Hunt, Emily Hunt, Lesley Ann Hunt, Nick Hunt, Karen Hurley, Kim Hurley, Nikki Hurley, Zack Hurley, Alan Ivey, Cathy James, John James, Cam Jamieson, Destiny Janes, Madeline Janes, Glynis Jenkins, Becky JM, Earl Johnston, Ashley Jones, Brianne Jordan, Zita Kavanagh-Taylor, Pea Kay, Karen Kearsey Hurley, Tonie Keats, Wendy Kelly, Peter Kelsey, Perry Kendall, Victoria Kenny, Steve Kent, Jacoub Khalid, Mona Khalil, Dave King, Eliza King, Heather King, Melanie Rebecca King, MK King, Sheena King, Steff King, Aimee Kinsella, Heather Kinsells, Ron Kinsella, Beth Knight, Wendy Koh, Gillian Lahey, SueAnne Lahey Oates, Sydney Lamswood, Paul Lane, Cez La Vie, Maria Lear, Sandra LeBlanc, Kim LeGrow, Ivy Lehr, Jo Lester, Shalane Lewis, Christine Lilly, Kelly Loch,

Brenda Lockyer, Carissa Lockyer, Marjorie Lockyer Hancock, Alyssa Lucas, Joanne Lundrigan, Ramona Lundrigan Sturge, Shjon Macdonald, Crystal Mahaney, Ashley Major, Michelle Major, Lawrence Mak, Ashley Marie, Kim Marsh, Megan Marshall, April Martin, Bob Martin, Janet Martin, Nicole Martin, Stephen Martin, Faith Mary, Miranda Mayo, Joanne McDonald, Rebecca McDonald, Erik McLean, Tina Mercer Barrett, Annette Dalc Michelin, Sherrie Molloy O'Brien, Susan Moore Piercey, Bev A. Morgan, Doris Morgan, Maxine Morgan, Michelle Morgan, Samantha Morgan, Seth Morgan, Emily Murphy, Jordan Murphy, Liam Murphy, Patricia E. Murphy, Steffy Murphy, Terry Murphy, Janice Murphy Williams, Yuri Muzychka, Vaida Nairn, Kelly Neville, Mary Neville, Michele Nicholson, Maureen A. Nolan, Melissa Nolan, Brenda Noseworthy, Ashleigh Oake, Melanie O'Brien, Robert O'Brien, Melissa O'Keefe, Linda O'Leary, Kathryn Oliver, Michelle Osborne, Annmarie Ottenheimer, Tyler Pardy, Cynthia Parsons, Reesa Parsons, Elsie Parsons-Collins, Melissa Parsons Edwards, Louise Pennell Howse, Barb Penton, Kerilyn Percy-Baldwin, Nicholas Perry, Samantha Piercey, Carla Pilgrim Mulrooney, Irel Pineda, John Pippy, Leanne Pitcher Webster, Laura Poirier, Kim Porter, Steve Porter, Brenda Power, Brendan Power, Charlene Power, Diane Power, Janet Power, Lori Power, Michelle Power, Tammy Power, Yvette Power, Patrina Power Murphy, David Powers, Melanie Preston, Joanne Pretty, Kathy Pretty, Kaylene Sara-Lee Pritchett, Trudy Puddicombe, Jennifer Purchase, Omar Farooq Rahman, Corinne Reid, Shelley Reid, Thelma Reid, Matthew Rice, Tiffany Richards, Colleen Richards Gosse, Terri-Lynn Rimmer, Becky Robbins, Kimmy Roche, Shawn Roche, Lori Roche, Irene Rodgers, Carl Rogers, Janine Rogers, Dina Rose, Jackie Rose, Julia Rose, Leanne Rossiter, Paul Rossiter, Steff Rowe, Theresa Rowsell, Melissa Ruby, Cyril Russell, Pauline Russell, Trina Russell, Michael Ryan, Alicia Sainsbury, Terry Scott, Julie Sears, Dana Sellars, Kim Shannahan, Lisa Marie Sharpe, Eddie Sheerr, Julie Sinnott, Grant Skiffington, Laura Skinner, Phyllis Skinner, Bob Smith, Jenna Smith, Karen Smith, Lori-Ann Smith, Margaret Smith Pauls, Pauline Snook, Courtney Snow, Kyle Snow, Kim Snow Hoskins, Noel Sooley, Jennifer Sparkes, Nadeen Sparks Chafe, Karleena Squires, Melanie Squires, Michelle Squires-Dawe, Stacey Squires Pittman, Elaine Simmons, Adina Stamp, Juanita Stamp, Alison Stanford, Darrell Steele, Maureen Steele, Courtney Stoodley, Susan Stuckless, Andrea Sullivan, Sandra Sweetland, Katy Tan, William Tan, Hope Taylor, Sharron Taylor Forristall, Bruce Templeton, Jeff Thistle, Charlene Tilley, Louise Tobin, Curtis Traverse, Kim Tremblett, Alick Tsui, Meagan Tucker, Diana Upshall, David Vere-Holloway, Sean Vinnicombe, Brad Wade, Sarah-Kay Walker, Kate Walsh, Patrick Walsh, Terri Walsh, Ashley Walsh-Newhook, Heather Walsh Rice, Desiree Walters, Holly Wareham, Matthew Wareham, Natalie Webber, Jonathan Wells, Sharon Whalen-Reeves, Stacey Wheeler, Tania Wheeler, Paul Whelan, Tim Whey, Brenda Williams, Cass Williams, Denise Williams, Janice Williams, Nikki Willmott, Robin Wiseman, Katherine Wiseman Ryan, Eileen Woodford, Mel Woodford, Delores Yarn, Jessica Young

Known affectionately as "Flanker the Third" by his grandmother, Margo Cranford, a.k.a. Mrs. Flanker, Nick Cranford was born and grew up in St. John's, Newfoundland. From crawling on his father's keyboard while he was working to helping Flanker Press reach the next level, Nick has been involved in every facet of the family publishing business.

When Snowmageddon 2020 struck Newfoundland, Nick created a Facebook group as a way to help his home province stay connected and make lasting memories. "NL Snowmageddon 2020 Warriors'' grew to over 100,000 members in just four days.

Nick is currently completing a business administration program at the College of the North Atlantic. His favourite pastimes include shooting, reading, and having a time with his friends.

Seen at the intersection of Hamilton Avenue and Patrick Street, St. John's, January 24
(Photo by Noel Harris)